# 101 THINGS TO DO FOR Christmas

# 101 THINGS TO DO FOR Christmas

Debbie Trafton O'Neal • Illustrated by Louise Comfort

HUNT & THORPE

Copyright © 1995 by *Hunt & Thorpe*
Text © *Debbie Trafton O'Neal*
Illustrations © *Louise Comfort*
Originally published by *Hunt & Thorpe 1995*
Designed by *The Bridgewater Book Company*

ISBN 1 85608 216 4

In Australia this book is published by:
*Hunt & Thorpe Australia Pty Ltd.*
9 Euston Street, Rydalmere NSW 2116

Write to

*Hunt & Thorpe*
Bowland House
off West Street, Alresford
Hants SO24 9AT

The right of Debbie Trafton O'Neal and Louise Comfort to be identified as
author and illustrator of this work has been asserted by them in accordance
with the Copyright, Designs and Patents Act 1988

A CIP catalogue record for this book is available from the British Library

Printed and bound in Hong Kong

# Contents

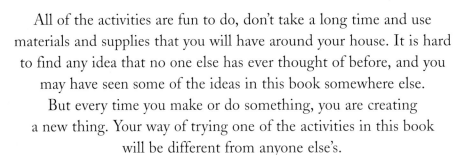

# Introduction

Christmas is a time of year when people all around the world are full of happiness, peace and love. Why? Because this is the holiday when we remember that God had a gift for us – the gift of baby Jesus. But sometimes it seems we are so busy getting ready for Christmas we forget to enjoy the moments we have.

*101 THINGS TO DO FOR CHRISTMAS* is a book full of good ideas and fun things to do to help you get ready and celebrate Christmas. There are ideas for gifts to make, good things to cook and bake, wrapping paper and tree trim ideas and much, much more!

All of the activities are fun to do, don't take a long time and use materials and supplies that you will have around your house. It is hard to find any idea that no one else has ever thought of before, and you may have seen some of the ideas in this book somewhere else. But every time you make or do something, you are creating a new thing. Your way of trying one of the activities in this book will be different from anyone else's.

*Here are some simple guidelines to help make this book easier to use:*

• **Always read the directions through at least once before you start, to make sure that you understand them**

• **Collect all of your materials and supplies before you start each project**

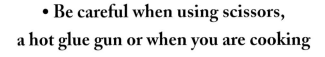

• **Be careful when using scissors, a hot glue gun or when you are cooking**

• **Be sure to ask an adult to help you with the specially marked projects**

• **Most importantly, have fun!**

# SHARING THE STORY

**1**

Over 2000 years ago, a man named Joseph and his wife, Mary, travelled many weary miles from their home to Bethlehem. At that time, Caesar Augustus had decreed that all people should return to their home town to be taxed. While Mary and Joseph were in Bethlehem, baby Jesus was born. Because there was no room for them in the inn, Mary and Joseph spent the night in a stable. Animals were the first creatures to welcome the new baby to the world, followed by the shepherds and the Wise Men from the east. Since that time, people everywhere celebrate the birth of Christ – the baby that changed the world – on December 25th.

# A is for Angel

C an you retell the Christmas story using the letters of the alphabet from A to Z? Make a special Christmas book that tells the story. Work on your A-B-C book a little bit each day and you will have it done by Christmas! Make a cover from heavier paper and share your book with your friends and family.

**2** Decide what each letter of the alphabet will stand for: e.g. A is for Angel, then print each title at the bottom of your page. Use your crayons or felt-pens to draw that part of the story.

**1** Cut out 8 sheets of paper so that when you fold them in half they will make the size of the book you want.

**3** Make a cover from heavier paper and tie the book together with a piece of coloured yarn.

## MATERIALS

White paper • crayons or felt-pens • heavier paper such as construction paper or cardboard for book covers • coloured yarn

# Christmas Story Box

## MATERIALS

A small box, such as a shoe box with a lid • scissors • crayons or felt-pens • assorted coloured paper pieces • glue or tape

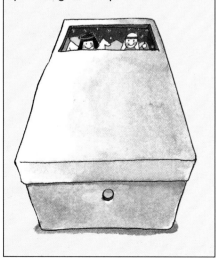

**1** Cut a peephole in one end of the box. Design the inside of your box to look like your favourite part of the Christmas story. If you want to show the stable where Jesus was born, colour the inside of the box to look like a barn. Colour the floor too.

**2** Draw, colour and cut out the animals, manger and people shapes. Fold a small strip of paper and glue it to the back of each figure so that it will stand up.

**3** Glue the figures to the floor of your box. Cut a rectangular strip from the lid of the box at the end opposite the peephole. Put the lid back and peek inside through the hole.

# Wallpaper Angel

**1** Trace and cut out the angel piece patterns from the wallpaper. Bend the body edges together to make a cone and leave a small opening at the top; glue the edges together.

**2** To make the head, fold the pipe cleaner in half and twist it into a loop with a

stem. Place the stem down into the cone and bend the loop over the top of the cone. Glue the loop to the top of the cone, then put a ring of glue on the loop and set the bead on top of it. If you want to, you can add a face with your felt-pen.

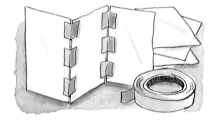

**3** Now fold the wings on the fold line and glue to the back of the body. Fold the arms into cones, too, and glue the straight edges together. Glue the arms to the sides of the body.

To add hair, spread a thin layer of glue onto the bead and stick on some curly yarn. You can add a small circle of silver or gold trim for a halo if you wish.

## MATERIALS

Wallpaper or other pretty paper pieces • pencil • scissors • glue • pipe cleaner (chenille wire) • wooden bead • felt-pen • curly yarn • silver or gold trim for a halo

# Accordion Story

## MATERIALS

Heavy paper cut into 7cm x 13cm rectangles • tape • crayons or felt-pens • ribbon or yarn

**1** Tape six pieces of paper together along the sides accordion style as the picture shows.

**2** Rewrite the Christmas story in six parts, carefully printing one part on each piece of paper. Then use your crayons or felt-pens to illustrate the story frames.

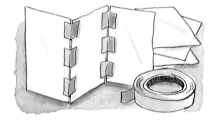

**3** When your drawings are done, tape a piece of ribbon or yarn to each outside page of the story. Fold the pages together accordion style and tie shut with the ribbon.

**4** Be sure to write a title and your name on the outside cover of your accordion storybook!

# Christmas Nativity

## MATERIALS

Paper plates or heavy paper cut into circles the size of dinner plates • scissors • tape or stapler • assorted colored paper scraps • crayons or felt-pens • trim scraps such as glitter, fabric, foil • cotton balls, etc. • pipe cleaners (chenille wires) • yellow paper scraps or straw

**1** The general directions for making this nativity with paper plates are to roll the plates into cone shapes and staple the cones along the overlapping edges in the back.

**2** Trim along the bottom curved edge of each figure, so that it will be able to stand on a table without falling over. Heads can be cut from paper scraps and taped or stapled to the bodies.

**3** To make animals, fold the plates in half and cut the curved edges into leg and body shapes as shown. Crease the folded edge carefully so that the figures will stand around the manger. Necks, heads and tails can be cut from paper scraps or other scrap materials and glued or stapled to the main bodies. Cotton balls or small scraps of fur will be nice if glued to the animal bodies. Pipe cleaners (chenille wires) can be bent into shepherds' staffs, arms and angels' halos.

**4** To make the manger, cut a plate in half and staple along the curved edges to make a pocket. Fill the manger with yellow paper scraps or straw.

**5** Cut a small sleeping baby shape from paper to be baby Jesus and put the baby into the manger. Tape the manger into the center of a table or display space.

**6** Spread more straw or paper scraps around the manger to represent the stable floor.

# Tree-top Angel

Paper plates and circles can make many different kinds of Christmas decorations. A tree-top angel with paper plate wings is fun and easy to do!

**1** First, roll the white paper into a cone shape and tape or staple it shut. Cut along the wide bottom edge to make sure that the cone will stand evenly.

**2** Use your scraps to cut a circle for the angel's head. Add a face with crayons or felt-pens and a halo from a scrap of foil or gold or silver trim.

**3** Cut the paper plate in half for wings and tape or staple to the back of the cone as shown.

## MATERIALS

One paper plate or piece of heavy paper cut into a plate-sized circle · white construction paper · tape or stapler · paper scraps · scissors · crayons or felt-pens · foil or gold or silver trim for a halo

# Story Symbol Wreath

## MATERIALS

A wreath made of straw or vines or a wreath shape cut from heavy cardboard · colored paper scraps · scissors · glue, tape or stapler · ribbon

Can you think of some of the symbols that make up the Christmas story? A star, donkey, manger, angel, shepherd, baby – all of these and more are symbols of the first Christmas when Jesus was born.

You can make a very special wreath to hang by your front door or in your house that will tell the Christmas story through symbols.

**1** Use your paper scraps and some of the shapes and patterns in this book to design your own symbols to hang on your wreath.

**2** Decorate and cut out your shapes, then attach them to your wreath with glue, tape or a stapler.

**3** Add a ribbon if you like!

# Paper Tube Nativity

**MATERIALS**

Cardboard tubes and paper rolls • coloured paper • scissors • glue or tape • fabric scraps • trim and other scraps • cotton balls • small stick

**1** To make the bodies, cover each tube with a different colour of construction paper. Cut face and hand shapes from paper and glue to the fronts of the tubes.

**3** Cut and glue fabric scraps to the tubes to make robes and head coverings. Wrap the tiniest tube in a scrap of fabric to make a blanket for the baby Jesus.

**2** To make a manger, cut a tube in half crosswise, then lengthwise. Round the sides, then glue the manger onto a smaller piece of cardboard tube as a base.

**4** Make the animals using the tube in a lengthwise position. Add cotton balls to the sheep's body. Make angel wings from white paper. Glue a star shape to a small stick and attach it to the back of the angel.

# Shadow Puppet Story

**MATERIALS**

Heavy paper • scissors • pencils or other sticks • tape • a bright light • a sheet or screen

A shadow puppet story of the first Christmas is fun to do!

**1** Cut simple figure shapes from heavy paper using some of the pictures in this book to give you an idea. All you need is the outline of the figure or shape so don't worry about colouring in any of the details.

**2** Tape a pencil or stick to the back of each figure when you are done. Practise telling the story by sitting behind a sheet or screen with a bright light shining from behind you to make a strong shadow on the screen.

# GIFTS TO GIVE

**2**

Perhaps the greatest excitement during the days of Christmas centres around the giving and receiving of gifts. Gift-giving on Christmas Day reminds us of the greatest gift that God gave us – the gift of his son, Jesus. As a way of sharing the joy we have because of Jesus' birth, it is especially fun to make gifts that we can give to other people.

# Two Pencil Toppers

## SNOWMAN

**I** Push one of the balls onto the pencil and glue into place. Roll the second ball in your hands to make it a little smaller, then glue to the first ball.

**2** Snip off a tip of the toothpick for the nose and push into the top ball. Glue two black beads above the nose and add three beads for a mouth.

**3** Cut the felt into a narrow strip and fringe the ends. Tie the scarf around the snowman's neck.

**4** Break two small twigs for arms and push into the snowman's body. Add more black beads for the snowman's buttons.

## PACKAGES

**I** Cut the foam pieces into small box shapes. Press the larger one (for the bottom package) into the pencil to make an indentation. Wrap both pieces of foam with the Christmas wrapping paper and glue them. Cut and tie small pieces of ribbon around each package and glue to the paper.

**2** Slit the paper around the indentation you have made and press the packages back onto the pencil. Glue the larger package to the pencil, then glue the smaller one on top. Use a pin pushed through the foam to hold the two packages together if needed.

## MATERIALS

You will need pencils for both pencil toppers • scissors • glue;
**Snowman –** two 2.5cm foam balls • toothpick • small black beads • a scrap of felt for the scarf • two small twigs
**Packages –** scraps of 2.5cm foam • scraps of Christmas paper • scraps of ribbon • pin

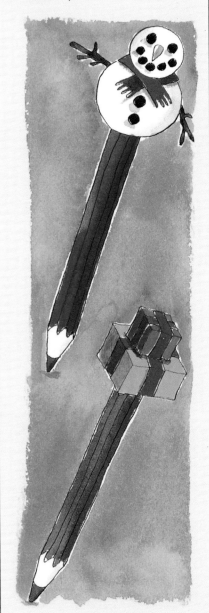

# Frame Ups

**1** Make sure the jar lids you are going to use are clean. Cut the photos so that they fit inside the lid and glue them in place.

**2** Tie your ribbon into a bow with streamers. If you want your bow to have 'wavy' ends, slide a piece of greaseproof paper under the ends of the ribbons and coat them with white glue. Arrange the 'waves' on the paper and let them dry.

**3** Remove the greaseproof paper and glue the bows and dried flowers to the tops of the jar lid photo frames. If you want to you can glue a magnet to the back of the jar lid to make it a picture that sticks on metal.

## MATERIALS

Clean jar lids • photos • ribbons • glue • greaseproof paper • small dried flowers • magnets (optional)

# Fingertip Frame

## MATERIALS

Wood or plastic picture frames • acrylic or other paint that dries quickly • a picture you have drawn that fits into the frame • wet towels for cleaning-up

**1** Paint the frame you have chosen in a variety of different colours. You might want to paint one side blue, one side yellow, one side red and one side green!

**2** After the paint dries, choose another colour of paint (like white) to make your fingertip prints with. Dip your fingertip into the paint and put dots all over the frame. When you are done, it might even look like it has snowed on your frame!

**3** When all of the paint has dried, put your picture inside the frame. Be sure to sign your name and the date on your artwork!

# Pet Treats

Y our pets will love this Christmas treat!

**1** Begin by making the treat moulds. You might make this mould in the shape of a heart or in the shape of a bone. Cut the cardboard into a strip that is 30cm long and 7cm wide. Cover it completely with the foil, then fold or bend the strip to make the shape that you want. Use a stapler to fasten the ends together. (You will need about 10 moulds to make this recipe.)

**2** Spray the baking sheet and the insides of the moulds with the cooking spray and place the moulds on the baking sheet.

**3** Mix 3 cups of dry pet food with enough warm water to cover it in the mixing bowl. Let it sit for several hours to make sure it is thoroughly moist. Some dog food can take longer – maybe even overnight.

**4** Then use your hands or a potato masher to mash up the pet food until it is like a thick dough. You can add more water if you think it needs it.

**5** Heat your oven to 350° Fahrenheit. Place 2 or more spoons of pet food mix into the moulds you have made, filling them up about 3.5 cm thick. Bake the pet treats for 30 to 60 minutes, or until they seem dry to touch. Turn off the oven, and let the treats cool in the oven for about 1 hour.

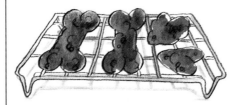

**6** Remove the moulds and let the treats cool and dry very well, so that they don't spoil. Pack the treats in a special bag and share them with all your furry friends!

## MATERIALS

Cardboard • aluminium foil • stapler • baking sheet • vegetable cooking spray or oil • dry cat or dog food that your pet likes • water • mixing bowl • spoon • potato masher

# Cat and Dog Treat Bags

You can make these special bags to store the pet treats you make for your friends with four legs and wagging tails, or use these bags for someone who especially likes dogs and cats!

## MATERIALS

Small brown or white paper bags • felt-pens • scissors • stapler • ribbon (optional)

**1** Use your felt-pens to draw the face of a cat or dog on your bag. With your scissors, trim the top to make the bag rounded (like your pet's head) and cut ears if you like. Be sure to write a special message on the bag!

**2** After you fill the bag up, you can staple it shut and add a ribbon if you like.

# Cat and Dog Pin-Ups

## MATERIALS

Both projects will need a wooden or plastic frame • a photo or picture you have drawn of your pet (or the pet of someone you are giving the picture to);
**Cat** – a mat board cut to fit into the frame • stamp pad and cat paw print stamp or a felt-pen
**Dog** – small dog bones or biscuits • glue • bow (optional)

### CAT FRAME

**1** If you want to make a frame for a favourite cat, be sure that the picture you have will show in the matted frame. Turn the mat board so that the white side is facing out, and stamp or draw paw prints all over it. Let the prints dry, then place the cat picture inside the frame.

### DOG FRAME

**2** For the dog frame, place your photo of your dog into the frame and make sure the glass is on it. Then spread a layer of glue around the edges to 'frame' the dog photo. Press dried dog bones or biscuits into the glue and let dry. Add a bow if you wish!

# Pretty Table Mats

laminating film. (Some libraries or book stores have machines that will do this for you.) This will protect your artwork and the table mats can be used and wiped clean!

## MATERIALS

White paper • watercolours • crayons or felt-pens • clear adhesive paper or laminating film • ribbon

**1** Use your imagination to draw one of your best pieces of artwork on the paper. You might want to try a combination of dots, squiggles and zig-zags! When you like your work, set it aside.

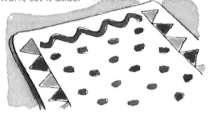

**2** When your artwork is dried, cover it on both sides with clear adhesive paper or

**3** A nice way to wrap these is to roll them up and tie them with a ribbon.

# Jingle Bell Socks

## MATERIALS

Assorted colours and sizes of socks • jingle bells or buttons • needle and thread • scissors

J ingle bell socks are a fun thing to make and give to a friend or a little sister! Grown-ups like them too!

**1** Decide where you want to sew the jingle bells or buttons – just around the top, up one side or scattered all over. Carefully stick your hand into the sock and sew the bell or button through several times.

**2** Make sure to knot the end well so that the bell doesn't fall off!

# Block Puzzles

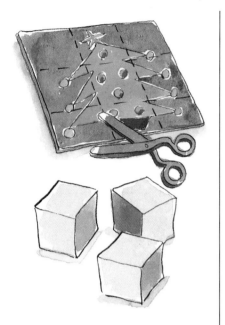

## MATERIALS

Wooden or plastic blocks (all the same size) • a picture or photo • scissors • rubber cement glue

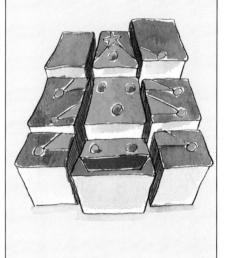

**1** Arrange the blocks with the smooth side up so that your photo or picture fits onto them exactly. Cut the picture so that each block will have one piece that fits it.

**2** Carefully spread rubber cement on the block and the picture piece, and glue them together.

**3** When the glue has dried, try the block puzzle to make sure that it works!

# Fancy Soap-Suds

*GET HELP!*

## MATERIALS

Different kinds of bars of soap • fabric scraps • ribbons • scissors • stickers or small pictures cut from magazines • paraffin or wax • double boiler • tongs

**1** For the fabric-wrapped soap, cut the fabric into a square that will fold nicely around the soap. Make sure that there is enough material to bring the four corners up and together at the top. Tie the corners with a pretty ribbon and you've finished.

**2** To make soap with a pretty picture, place a sticker or small picture you have cut out from a magazine onto the bar of soap. (If you wet the soap with a wet finger, the picture will stick.)

**3** Then, with a grown-up's help, melt the paraffin or wax in a double boiler and dip the soap into the paraffin, holding the picture side down. Now the picture is sealed on.

# Sock Puppets

## MATERIALS

Old or mis-matched socks ·
buttons · yarn · scissors · pom-
pom yarn balls · needle and thread
· scraps of felt · glue

You can make fun sock puppets from socks and scraps you have around the house.

**1** Collect the materials together. Roll the cuff of the sock up and try it on your hand to see if it fits well.

**2** Decide where you will sew buttons for eyes. Add a yarn pom-pom for the nose, and if your puppet needs whiskers, sew yarn to the end of the sock.

**3** If you don't want to do a lot of sewing on your puppet, glue felt scraps to the sock to make the face.

# Note Pad Reminder

Everyone needs to make a list or keep a note. This reminder note pad holder makes a great gift.

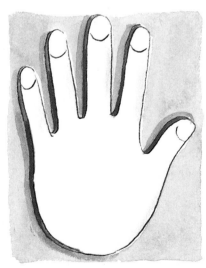

**1** Trace the shape of a hand (maybe your own) onto the thin cardboard. Use your felt-pen to add details – like fingernails – to make the hand look real. Cut out the hand.

**2** Tie a ribbon or yarn bow around the index finger as a "reminder" symbol.

**3** Glue the pad of paper to the centre of the hand print, and glue or tie another piece of ribbon or yarn to the back or corner. Attach your pencil to this hand and presto! Everything you need to make yourself a note is here.

## MATERIALS

Heavy paper, such as posterboard or thin cardboard · felt-pens · yarn or ribbon · a small note pad or paper · glue · a pencil

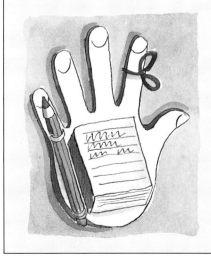

# Pressed Flower Candles

## MATERIALS

Flowers and leaves you have collected and pressed flat • paraffin or wax • double boiler • candles • tweezers • a paint brush • tissue paper

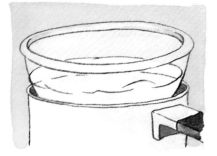

**1** Melt the paraffin or wax in a double boiler. Remember, this is a job you should do with a grown-up!

**2** Carefully arrange the pressed flowers and leaves onto the candle.

**3** Use a small brush to paint the wax over the flowers. When the wax is cooled, wrap the candles in tissue paper to store.

# Holiday Photo Album

**1** Cover the album or scrapbook by placing the album in the centre of a piece of wrapping paper or a map.

**2** Fold the edges of the paper so that it fits the album, then glue them down.

**3** If you like, print a title for the book, such as 'My Holiday' on the front cover. You might want to make an album with a special wrapping paper, such as Christmas paper, to keep pictures from your family's Christmas holidays. Cover the entire album with clear self-adhesive paper to protect it.

## MATERIALS

Photo album or scrapbook • map or other wrapping paper • glue • clear self-adhesive paper

# Cotton Reel Doll

**1** Paint three cotton reels for the doll's shirt. Paint the other four cotton reels for the doll's trousers.

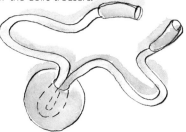

**2** After the paint dries, fold the cord in half and push the folded end into the bead and glue in place. Wrap masking tape around the ends of the cord so that it is easy to thread into the spools and beads.

**3** Thread each end of the cord through one arm cotton reel and a 2cm bead, and then back through the arm. Thread both ends through the main body cotton reel, then thread each end through the 2 leg cotton reels so that you end with a bead and a large knot on the end. Add a face to the bead head and glue yarn on for hair if you like.

### MATERIALS

Seven 4cm wooden or plastic cotton reels • paints • brushes • 75cm of string or cord • a 3.5cm wooden bead with a hole halfway through for the head • glue • scraps of yarn • four 2cm wooden beads • masking tape

# Funny Face Bath Mitts

GET HELP!

### MATERIALS

One flannel face cloth for each mitt • needle and thread • scissors • fabric scraps • glue

**1** Fold the face cloth in half and have a grown-up help sew the edges to make a mitt. Decide on the kind of face you want the bath mitt to have. Will it have ears? whiskers? a heart-shaped nose?

**2** Cut the shapes from fabric and glue or sew to your funny face bath mitt. You might want to add some bubble bath or soap to the mitt when you give it for a gift.

# Woven Bookmark

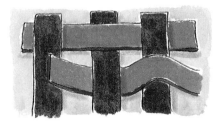

**1** Decide which colours of paper or ribbon you would like your bookmark to be. Choose 5 or 6 pieces to start with (depending on how wide you want the bookmark to be). Lay the pieces out and begin weaving back and forth, leaving the ends free until your bookmark is done.

**2** When you like your design, carefully place a dot of glue on the edge of each

strip to hold it in place. You can leave the ends free or cut them off if you like.

**3** If you want to, cut a heart or other shape, or the initial of someone's name from paper to glue to the bottom of the bookmark.

# Name Puzzle

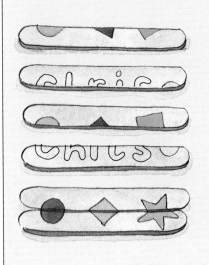

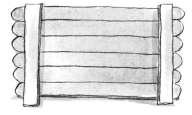

**1** Lay six wooden sticks per name side by side (see the drawing) on a table or flat surface. Tape the ends together just to hold the sticks in place while you decorate them.

**2** Carefully print your friend's name across all of the sticks with a felt-pen using bold

lettering. Add other decorations to your design if you like.

**3** Remove the tape and try to put the puzzle back together! Put the pieces in an envelope or small box to give as a gift.

# WRAP IT UP

**H**alf of the fun of receiving a gift is wondering what will be inside the special box or bag.

# Shapes to Make

First decide how big an envelope you will need to make for the size of the gift you are giving. Think about the shape you want your envelope to be. Will it be a square or rectangle? A heart? A Christmas tree? An envelope that looks like a letter?

**1** Cut two pieces of paper together to make the shape you decide on exactly the same size. If you are going to add any decorations or designs to the envelope, use your felt-pen to do this before you close the envelope up.

**2** Begin stapling or taping the edges of the envelope together, but before you finish, slip your gift inside. Then finish stapling the edges together. Add a ribbon and gift tag if you wish.

## MATERIALS

Assorted kinds of paper to make different envelopes • scissors • felt-pens • tape or a stapler • ribbon or gift tag (optional)

# Reindeer and Mouse Bags

## MATERIALS

Paper bags of all sizes • scissors • paper scraps • glue or tape • felt-pens • stapler • pom-pom

You can hide your Christmas presents in an animal bag.

## REINDEER BAG

**1** Fold the top edge of the bag over and crease it. Draw facial features or cut them from scraps of paper and add them to the bag. Cut ears or antlers from other scraps of paper. You might even want to make the antlers with your handprints!

## MOUSE BAG

**2** Make a mouse bag by folding one corner of the bag to make a triangular head. Staple the bag shut and add cut-out paper ears, a tail and an eye. Draw whiskers on the mouse and add a pom-pom for the nose!

# Cracker Tubes

## MATERIALS

Paper tubes • fabric or wrapping paper • tape • ribbon or yarn

For very small gifts, it is easy to make cracker tubes in which to hide the presents.

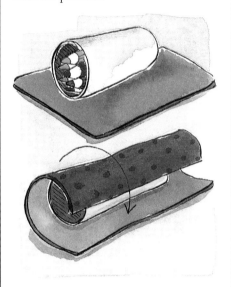

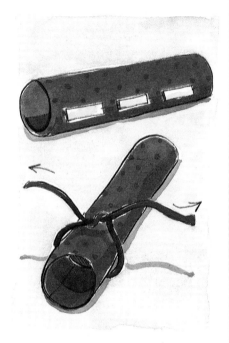

**1** Place the item inside the paper tube. Roll paper or fabric around the tube. When the tube is all covered, tape it shut.

**2** Tie the ends of the paper with ribbon or yarn as shown, or press them inside, into the tube.

# Fabric Bags

If you are concerned about recycling and caring for the earth, you might want to make fabric bags that you and your family can use for many Christmases! If you think ahead, you can find pretty Christmas fabric to use for making Christmas bags for next year!

## MATERIALS

Pretty fabrics and materials • scissors • a sewing machine or needle and thread • ribbons

**1** Start by folding and cutting your fabric to make a bag. If you fold your material right, you will only have to sew up two sides to make your bag.

**2** Sew your bag up, then put the gift inside and tie the top with a pretty ribbon.

# Paper Horns

## MATERIALS

Large sheets of heavy paper • tape or stickers • felt-pens • glue and glitter • tissue paper (optional)

**1** You might wrap your gift in tissue paper first before you begin rolling the paper into a cone shape.

**2** Lay the gift you are wrapping in the centre of the paper and begin rolling

one side to make the paper into a cone shape. It will start to look something like an ice-cream cone as you are rolling. Each time you wrap a gift this way, the finished package will look a little bit different.

**3** You might want to fold the ends in and tape them shut so that the package is secure. Decorate your horn.

# Edible Boxes

Cakes and biscuits can form the base for gift boxes that you can eat!

**1** Lay the bottom biscuit piece on a flat surface and spread a stripe of icing along each side.

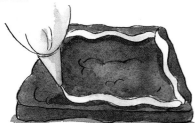

**2** While the icing is still moist, press another biscuit into it to form the sides.

**3** Hold the biscuit in place until the icing is set and stiff. You may find that it will help to set the ends of the box in slightly (not in perfect line) with the other sides. After the icing sets, use the remaining icing and small sweets to decorate the box. You could even decorate another biscuit for the box lid!

## MATERIALS

Square or rectangular-shaped cakes or biscuits • icing • assorted small sweets and 'sprinkles' for the decoration

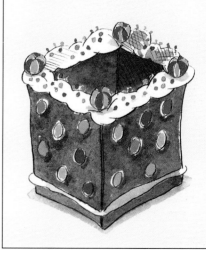

# Three Fancy Wraps

Who said you need to buy wrapping paper for your Christmas packages? Look around your house – there are already many things there that you can use – the sky's the limit!

## RECYCLED PAPER WRAP

Newspaper, comics and black and white print make nice wrapping paper. Use your stamps or markers to make designs on the paper. Tie it with a colourful ribbon and write who the gift is for on the paper with felt-pens.

## BROWN PAPER BAGS

Brown paper bags also make great gift wraps! Not only can you cut shapes out (see *page 25*) you can cut apart and decorate the bags with paints, felt-pens and stamps. A bright ribbon or piece of yarn makes a nice bow.

## ARTWORK WRAP

Grandmas and Grandpas like to get pieces of your artwork, and when it hides a special gift at Christmas time they will be especially happy!

## THE FINISHING TOUCH

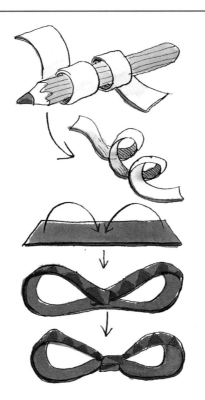

How about bows? If you cut narrow strips of brown or white paper and then stamp designs on them, the strips can be curled and looped to make bows and package trims.

## MATERIALS

Newspaper and comics • tissue paper • wallpaper and other assorted types of papers • brown paper bags • paints • felt-pens • stamp pads • ribbon or yarn

# Three Fancy Jars

I f you are giving someone a gift of a special recipe, bath powder, or an unusual-shaped gift, a jar can make a good package and a gift itself for the person to use afterwards. Make sure the jars are clean and dry before you start.

## PET FRIENDS

You might paint or stamp paw prints on your jar and fill it with animal biscuits for your pet-loving friend.

## A RECIPE FOR SUCCESS

If you are putting cocoa mix in your jar, be sure to add the recipe for how much cocoa to put into each cup of hot water. Maybe you can add a small bag of marshmallows.

## WRAP AROUND

Wrap pieces of fat yarn or ribbon around and around the jar until you reach the top. Tie the ends in a bow. (You might find that you need to add a few drops of glue to the jar and yarn here and there.)

## THE FINISHING TOUCH

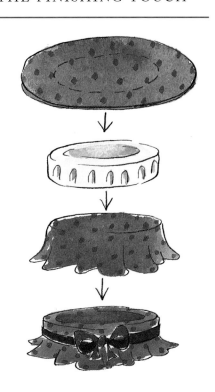

Cut a circle of fabric and glue it to the jar lid. Make sure that the circle hangs down enough so that you can make it into a ruffle and tie it on the jar with ribbon or yarn.

## MATERIALS

A variety of glass and plastic jars with tops or corks to fit the tops • paints • stamp pads and stamps • ribbon or yarn • glue • fabric scraps

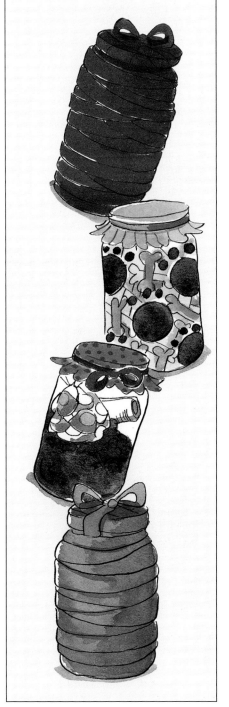

# Laced and Stapled Shapes

## MATERIALS

Large pieces of colourful paper · scissors · paper hole punch · yarn or string · stapler

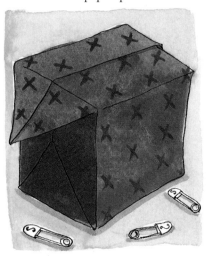

**1** For hard-to-wrap presents that are odd shapes and sizes, draw simple shapes such as a sugar cane, star or crown on the paper.

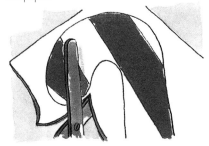

**2** Cut two shapes out together, then punch holes around the edges.

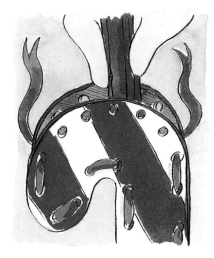

**3** Slip the gift inside and then lace it together around the edges with yarn or string. It is fun to make a laced shape that gives a hint about what is hiding inside!

If your paper shape is very unusual or hard to lace, you can also staple the shape all around the edges to fasten it together.

# Fabric Wraps

S ometimes a gift is so hard to wrap that a piece of fabric or material makes the best 'paper' possible!

**1** Boxes and square items can be easily wrapped using the fabric as if it were paper. A piece of tape or a pin will hold the edges together.

**2** You could try combining the fabric for a gift wrap and bow. Lay out the fabric so that it is smooth on a table. Set the gift in the centre and fold the side edges in towards the centre, overlapping them so that the gift is covered up.

**3** Then fold the other two sides in towards the centre, tying the ends in the middle to fasten the package and make the bow.

## MATERIALS

Pieces of fabric or materials · scissors · tape · pins · ribbon or yarn

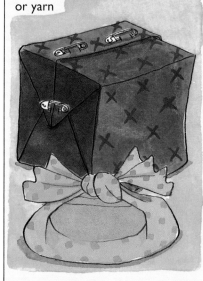

# Tambourine and Maraca

Two paper plates of the same size • tape • streamers or ribbons • jingle bells • paperclips • pennies or beans • stapler • tissue paper • empty juice cans • paper • felt-pens

F or a very small gift, you can make a tambourine or maraca that will be fun to play with and fun to open too!

## TAMBOURINE

I Tape the small gift in the centre of one of the plates and make sure it is secure.

2 Decorate the outsides of both of the paper plates with streamers, ribbons and jingle bells.

3 Put the two plates together, placing a handful of beans, paperclips, etc. inside and then staple all of the edges together. Make sure the staples are close enough together so that the paperclips don't fall out! This gift is fun to shake and unwrap.

## MARACA

I Tape paper to one outside edge of the can and then roll it all around the can so that it is covered.

2 Add decorations if you wish. You could use felt-pens or ribbons.

3 Place a handful of pennies, beans, etc. inside the can. Seal the open end of the can with a circle of paper. Write the person's name on the maraca and watch them enjoy the surprises inside!

# TRIM THE TREE

**4**

Bringing a Christmas tree into your house is perhaps the part of Christmas that is the most fun! It is fun to decorate a tree that is part of God's creation, and you can be creative yourself when you try making some of the ornaments and tree trims that you will find in this chapter.

GET HELP!

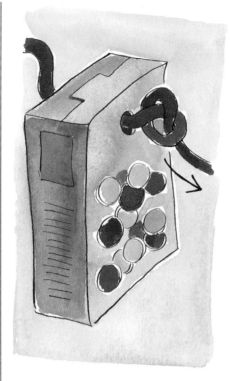

**MATERIALS**

Red and green yarn · scissors · collection of sweet boxes · selection of sweets and lollipops · pencil to make holes in the boxes

**1** Cut some red and green yarn to the length you want for your garland. Ask a grown-up to poke a hole in either end of the sweet boxes. Then arrange your sweets and lollipops with the boxes in a pleasing design.

**3** Pull the yarn through the box to the opposite side, then tie a double knot as before.

**2** To begin stringing the pieces together, push one end of the yarn through the holes in a box. Tie a double knot in the yarn next to the hole in the box to keep it from sliding.

**4** Continue stringing your sweets and lollipops and then add more sweet boxes as you have designed. Tie an extra sturdy knot at the end and twine your garland around your tree.

# Clothespeg Snowman

**1** Glue three white pom-poms or cotton wool balls to one side of the clothespeg.

**2** Cut a black hat from felt or sturdy fabric and glue to the snowman's head. Make

paper circles from black paper with a paper punch and glue on to make the snowman's eyes and buttons.

**3** Glue a snip of yarn on for the snowman's mouth. Plait three short pieces of red yarn to make the snowman's scarf and glue on. The snowman can sit or be clipped onto your Christmas tree's branches.

## MATERIALS

Clothespin · three white pom-poms or cotton wool balls · black felt or sturdy fabric · glue · black paper · paper punch · red yarn

# Angel

## MATERIALS

Clothespeg · coloured felt for angel's dress and wings · white paper · glue · glitter or ribbon (optional) · yarn

**1** Follow the basic instructions for the clothespeg snowman, but cut a triangle piece of felt or fabric for the angel's body.

**2** Cut white wings from felt and glue the body and wings to the clothespeg. Add glue and glitter or ribbon trim to the angel's dress if you like.

**3** Cut a round paper face for the angel and draw eyes and a mouth. Add fluffy yarn to the top of the angel's head for hair.

# Animal Danglers

O n the night of Jesus' birth, the first creatures to share the good news with Mary and Joseph were the animals in the stable. Perhaps that is why we remember to take extra-special care of the animals in our lives during the Christmas season!

Even though the first animals to see Jesus may not have been lions and tigers and bears, and the animals that you take care of will probably be more like cats and dogs and rabbits, it is still fun to add animal crackers to your Christmas tree decorations! The best part of these tree-trimmers is that you can eat them throughout the Christmas season!

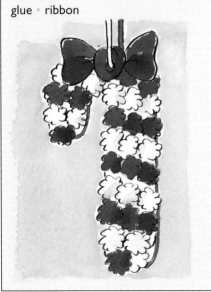

**1** Choose the animal biscuits that you want to hang on your tree. (Maybe you can eat the broken ones first!)

**2** Carefully poke a pin or needle into the top part of the cracker back as shown (ask a grown-up for help). Thread a piece of clear thread or string through the hole.

**3** Tie a knot after each animal to stop them from slipping and hang from the tree.

## MATERIALS

Box of animal biscuits • pin or needle • clear thread or string

# Pom-pom Sugar Canes

## MATERIALS

Thin cardboard • red and white pom-poms or cotton wool balls • glue • ribbon

**1** Cut a sugar cane shape from thin cardboard.

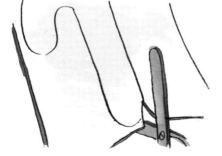

**2** Choose red and white pom-pom or cotton wool balls to cover the cardboard in a red-white-red-white pattern.

**3** Spread a thin layer of glue on the sugar cane shape and press the pom-poms on it. After the glue dries, you can add a ribbon bow if you like. Hang your sugar cane from the tree for everyone to see!

# Ping-Pong Snowman

1 Glue the two ping-pong balls together and let them dry. Use a black felt-pen to draw a face and buttons on the snowman.

2 Cut a circle of black felt for the hat and glue it to the top of his head.

3 Cut a rectangle of black felt to roll around and glue on the top of the circle as the top part of the hat. Tie a piece of the striped ribbon around the snowman's 'neck' and attach a piece of thread for hanging.

# Pasta Twirls

1 Spread greaseproof paper to work on so that the glue and pasta do not stick to the working surface.

2 Move the various pasta shapes around on the greaseproof paper, using some of these designs to give you ideas.

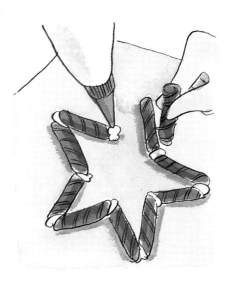

3 When you are happy with a design that you have made, glue the pasta pieces in place and let dry. When dry, carefully peel away any greaseproof paper that may be sticking to the pasta twirl, attach a piece of thread and hang from the tree.

# Felt Stockings

perhaps adding a cuff or a toe and heel of a different colour. You could write someone's name or initials on the stocking with a felt-pen or by gluing a piece of ribbon to it.

**MATERIALS**

Your favourite colour of felt or another sturdy fabric • paper for a pattern • scissors or pinking shears • needle and thread or glue • buttons • ribbon • felt-pen

**I** Cut a double piece of felt or other fabric in a stocking shape. Sew or glue the stocking edges together.

**2** Use bits of ribbon, buttons or other fabric to add detail to the stocking,

**3** If you can attach a piece of ribbon to the top of the stocking, it could hang from your Christmas tree.

# Fancy Paper Fan

**MATERIALS**

One 18cm x 35cm piece of gift wrap or other paper for each fan • glue • lace or other fancy trim

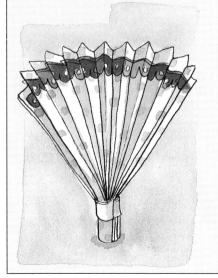

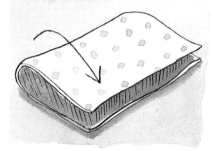

**I** Cut the paper so that the size is 18cm x 35cm. Fold the paper in half, lengthwise, with the right side out.

**2** Glue lace across one side of the paper, close to the edge that is folded. Then

begin folding the paper back and forth in 1cm wide accordion pleats.

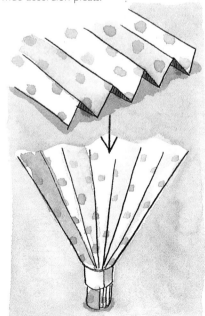

**3** Tape the bottom closed and add other decorative trim if you like.

# Woven Paper Ornaments

**1** Cut the coloured paper into 2.5cm strips. Fold the white paper in half and cut slits from the folded edge to within 5cm of the opposite side.

**2** Open the white paper and begin weaving the coloured paper strips over

and under, until you have woven the piece entirely. Glue the papers together in each loose place with rubber cement or a dot of glue.

**3** When dry, trace simple shapes like a star, tree, or sugar cane onto the woven paper. Cut out the shape, and glue any loose edges that might curl up. Punch a hole in the top, attach a thread and hang from the Christmas tree.

## MATERIALS

Heavy paper in white and two other colours • scissors • rubber cement or other glue • pencil • paper hole punch • thread

# Ice-cream Cones

## MATERIALS

Ice-cream cones • glue • old glass or plastic Christmas tree balls

**1** Run a strip of glue along the top edge of an ice-cream cone.

**2** Place the glass or plastic ball onto the cone – making sure it is upright.

**3** Hold it in place until the glue has started to dry. Make sure the hanger for the ornament is centred at the top. Attach a piece of thread and hang from a high branch on your tree.

# Lace Chain Garlands

## MATERIALS

Pieces of lace and other sewing trim • scissors • glue

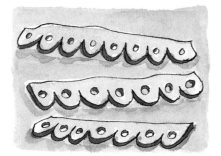

1 Cut the lace or trim into even lengths, about 13–20cm.

2 Glue the ends of one piece of lace together. Then, just as you make a paper chain, attach the ends of another piece of lace through the first chain link.

3 Continue in this way until you have made a garland long enough for your tree, or until you run out of lace!

# Vegetable Basket Ornaments

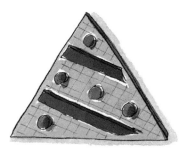

1 Cut a triangular tree shape from a piece of the vegetable basket. Decorate the tree with bits of ribbon, felt and other colourful fabrics.

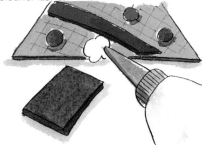

2 Cut a tree trunk from brown paper and glue to the base of the tree.

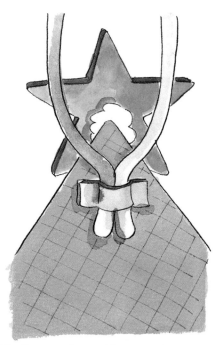

3 Cut a star from gold paper and glue to the top of the tree. Attach a loop of yarn at the top to hang the ornament.

## MATERIALS

Vegetable baskets made from plastic or cane • ribbon, felt and fabric • glue • scissors • scraps of brown paper • gold paper • yarn

# Cork Animal Ornaments

## MATERIALS

Corks in assorted shapes and sizes • a sharp knife (to use with an adult's help) • glue • felt-pens • ribbon

**1** Arrange several corks into different animal shapes. Glue the corks in place when you like the animal you have made. Use felt-pens to make the face and other features on the cork, adding swirls and curls to suggest fur if you like.

**2** Once the glue has dried completely, tie a ribbon around your animal's neck and add a ribbon tie at the top for hanging.
 If you need to cut the corks to make your animal, ask an adult for help.

# Spirals and Spinners

## MATERIALS

Metallic pipe cleaners (chenille wires)

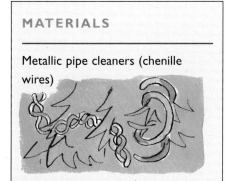

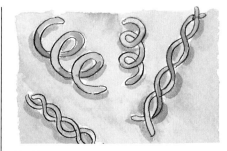

**1** Select some pipe cleaners of different colours and sizes.

**2** Twist the pipe cleaners into spirals and let them wind their way through your Christmas tree!

# Lacy Heart

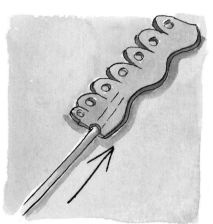

## MATERIALS

2.5cm lace • 35cm of florists' wire • ribbon

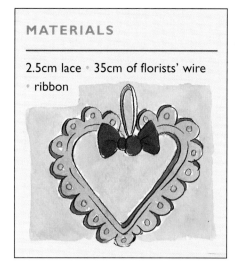

**1** Thread the lace onto the wire, then bend the wire into a heart shape.

**2** Add a bow at the top and a ribbon tie for hanging on your tree.

# Curly Bearded St Nick

I  Copy the shapes shown here and cut them from construction paper.

2  Glue the main body shapes together, adding smaller details with paper scraps or felt-pens. Glue a pom-pom to his hat. Add the white beard to St Nick and cut slits from the bottom up.

3  Use a pencil to curl his paper beard. When all of the glue has dried, attach a thread to the pom-pom on St Nick's hat to hang him from your Christmas tree.

## MATERIALS

White, pink and red construction paper • pencil • scissors • glue • felt-pens • pom-pom • thread for hanging

# Ribbon Pinwheels

## MATERIALS

Plaid ribbon 7cm wide • scissors • glue • one 6cm cardboard circle for each ornament • thread

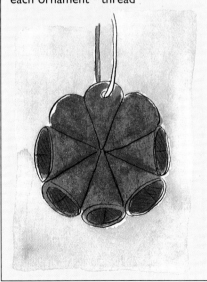

I  Cut the ribbon into triangles (experiment with the size until you find one that you like best). Roll the triangles together to make cone shapes and glue together.

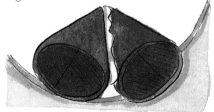

2  Begin gluing the ribbon cones with the smaller points facing into the centre of the circle.

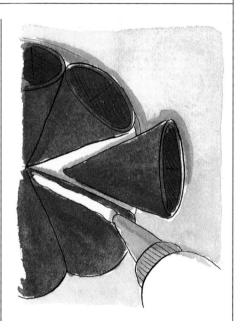

3  Continue until you have filled the entire circle. The finished ornament will look like a sunburst or a pinwheel. Attach a thread for hanging this pinwheel from your Christmas tree.

# Popcorn Hearts

1 Draw a heart shape on the thin cardboard and cut the heart shape out.

2 Spread a thin layer of glue on the heart and gently press popped popcorn over the glue, covering all of the cardboard.

3 Tie the red ribbons into bows, and attach to the heart. Use a longer red ribbon for hanging from a tree branch.

## MATERIALS

Thin cardboard · pencil · scissors · glue · popped popcorn · red ribbon

# Craft Stick Sled

## MATERIALS

Seven or more craft or popsicle sticks for each sled · glue · felt-pens · ribbon or yarn

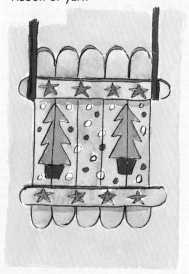

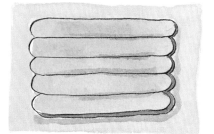

1 Make sure the sticks you are using are clean and dry. Lay five or more sticks side by side and glue them together.

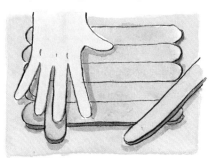

2 When the glue dries, lay two other sticks across the ends to form the crossbars of the sled. (If you want to use bigger sticks, or make a bigger sled, you can use more sticks than this.)

3 When the glue dries, use felt-pens to draw designs on the sticks and decorate the sled. Tie ribbon to the top crossbar for hanging the sled from your Christmas tree.

# Cotton Reel Ornaments

## MATERIALS

Plastic or wooden cotton reels • ribbon or fabric scraps • glue • Christmas wrapping paper scraps • other kinds of sewing or craft trim • ribbon

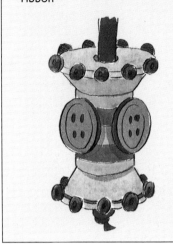

**1** Collect your materials together. Glue a piece of ribbon, fabric or Christmas wrapping paper around the outside of the cotton reel.

**2** Use other bits and pieces of trim and decorations to add to the cotton reel. When you like your cotton reel ornament, tie a ribbon to the top for hanging.

# Folded Paper Chains

## MATERIALS

Scraps of Christmas wrapping paper or other pretty paper scraps • scissors

This paper chain is a fun one to make and you can keep adding to it year after year after year!

**1** Cut the paper into pieces that are 5cm x 7cm. Fold the paper pieces in half lengthwise and reopen. Fold each long edge to crease it and then fold together on the crease to make a narrow strip.

**2** Now fold in half crosswise and reopen, then fold the short ends to crease. Fold in half along the crease and the strip should now form a V.

**3** With the singly folded edges facing up, slide the ends of the V of one piece through another piece and pull together to secure. Repeat, adding enough V-shaped pieces to complete your garland.

# Baby Jesus in a Blanket

## MATERIALS

Scraps of flannel or other soft fabric • scissors • peanuts in the shell • glue • felt-pen • yarn or ribbon

**1** Cut the flannel into a square that is about 5cm x 5cm. Glue a peanut in the shell to the centre of the flannel and add a face with a felt-pen.

**2** When the glue has dried, wrap the ends of the blanket around the peanut as if it were a baby and glue them shut.

**3** Attach a loop of yarn or ribbon for hanging from the Christmas tree.

# Sugar Cane Hearts

**1** Collect your materials, then lay a piece of greaseproof paper flat on a table.

**2** Place two sugar canes face to face to make a heart shape on the paper. Glue the sugar canes together.

**3** When the glue has dried, carefully peel the greaseproof paper away. Tie a ribbon bow at the top.

## MATERIALS

Greaseproof paper • two small sugar canes for each ornament • glue gun or craft glue • ribbon

# Postage Stamp Stars

**1** Glue cancelled postage stamps to the cardboard, overlapping them to make sure that the cardboard is covered.

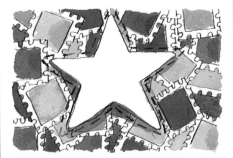

**2** Cut a star shape from paper and lay over the stamp design, tracing around it.

**3** Cut the stamp star out then cut another exact shape to fit onto the back. Attach thread for hanging.

## MATERIALS

Cancelled postage stamps • glue • thin cardboard • pencil • paper • scissors • thread

# Glittery Shells

## MATERIALS

Shells you have collected • glue • glitter • ribbon

Your Christmas tree can also be a reminder of the good times you had while you were on a summer holiday at the beach!

**1** Carefully trace with glue some of the ridges and designs on your shells.

**2** Sprinkle glitter over them. Then shake off the excess glitter and let dry.

**3** Tie a ribbon loop and glue to the shell to let it hang from your Christmas tree.

# GREETINGS TO SEND

*5*

*W*hat fun it is to receive cards and letters every day of the year, but especially during the season of Christmas time. And sending Christmas greetings to celebrate the joy of Jesus' birth is as much fun as opening the post yourself! Have fun with some of the different ways to share a Merry Christmas with your friends near and far.

## MATERIALS

Photo or picture you want to send • pencil • sharp scissors • ruler • thin cardboard or posterboard • rubber cement glue • felt-pens • envelope to fit the size of the puzzle card

**1** Decide what shapes you will cut your puzzle card into. You might want to cut squares, rectangles or crazy shapes. Lightly draw your design to cut out on the back of the photo, using the ruler to help you make the straight lines even. If your photo seems very thin and curls up at the edges, you can use the rubber cement to glue the photo to the thin cardboard before you trace your puzzle shape.

**3** Cut the photo into pieces. Make sure you follow the pencil lines.

**2** If there is room on the back of your picture, you can print a Christmas message such as 'Celebrate the Season of Jesus' Birth!' or 'Merry Christmas from me to you' on the back of the card before you cut it out. This way there will be a two-sided puzzle that the person who receives it can put together.

**4** When you are happy with your puzzle card, slip the pieces into the envelope, address it and send your greetings on their way.

1 Cut a strip of paper with the tabs as shown.

2 Divide the strip evenly into four squares and inside each square mark a border all the way around it.

3 Inside each square, draw a simple Christmas symbol shape, such as a tree, star, manger, camel or snowman. Make sure to draw the shape so that it is attached to the border at several points.

4 With sharp scissors cut out the areas around the shape, between the border and the centre shape.

5 Glue a strip of tissue paper or cellophane inside the paper strip to cover the entire inside. With the needle, carefully poke two small holes on opposite sides of the square – you might ask a grown-up for help.

6 Tie the thread as shown. Carefully fold your shadow cube into four sections, with directions to the recipient if you think he or she will need them. To finish the cube, the tabs will need to be glued together so that the shape of the strip becomes a cube.

## MATERIALS

One 13cm x 50cm strip of paper cut as shown in the drawing with tabs • ruler • pencil • scissors • glue • tissue paper or cellophane • needle • fine thread• envelope

# Postcard Dots

## MATERIALS

Standard-sized postcards • pencil •
sticker dots or dots from the scraps
made when using a paper hole
punch • glue

**1** Lightly sketch a design that you want on
the front of your postcard.

**2** If you have dot stickers, use them to
outline or fill in the shape of your design.

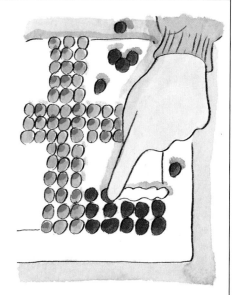

**3** If you are using paper dots and glue,
spread a thin line of glue along the edge
of the design and press the dots into it. Fill in
the shape with glue and dots too if you wish.
You can even use dots to write your holiday
greeting!

# Cut Paper Cards

**1** To begin with, cut an assortment of
paper shapes – squares, circles, triangles,
ovals, rectangles and any other shapes that
you would like to work with. (If you are
feeling brave, you can even try tearing the
paper to make interesting shapes!)

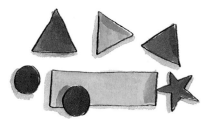

**2** Lay out several different shapes and
move them around on your work table,
trying to form them into a picture using the
shapes. Use some of the pictures in this book
to give you ideas. Can you make a stable and
star? How about a camel or three crowns?

**3** When you are pleased with your design,
glue the shapes onto the card. Carefully
print your message on the card with felt-
pens, and when the glue is dry it will be
ready to send.

## MATERIALS

A variety of paper scraps • scissors
• clean white paper folded into
standard card size • glue • felt-pens
• envelopes

# Quilted Greetings

Use some of the ideas in this book to get you started thinking about a favourite quilt design. You might want to make a star or other symbol that reminds you of Christmas.

I Draw your quilt patterns on heavy paper and cut out. Place the patterns on the fabrics you have chosen, trace around them, and then cut the fabric.

2 Spread a thin layer of glue onto your card and place the quilt pieces on it.

3 When the glue has dried, use your felt-pen to trace small lines around the edge of the quilt pattern, making it look like stitching. Use the felt-pens to write your message inside the card too!

## MATERIALS

Heavy paper for patterns • scissors felt-pens • fabric scraps • glue • folded paper for cards • envelopes

# Lacing Cards

## MATERIALS

Heavy paper such as posterboard • pencil • scissors • paper hole punch • felt-pens • yarn or ribbon • envelope

I Trace simple shapes, such as a stocking, snowman, star or gift box, onto the heavy paper. Cut out the shapes. Use the paper hole punch to make holes around the edges of your shape, trying to space them evenly around each side.

2 Print a holiday message in the centre of the shape with felt-pens.

3 Thread one end of the yarn or ribbon through several of the holes around the edge to lace the shape.

# Pin-point Pretties

**1** Use one of the designs in this book as your pattern for a pin-point card. Trace the general outline of the shape on the pattern paper, then tape the pattern over the card paper.

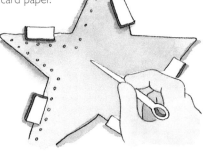

**2** Use the thick sewing needle to carefully prick holes around the edge of the

pattern. Try to make the holes as evenly spaced as possible.

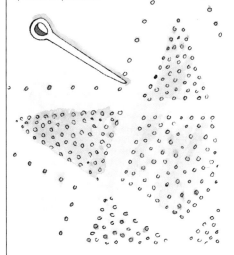

**3** Once you have pricked the holes around the edge of the design, remove the pattern paper. You might want to fill in parts of the design with holes, too. When you are done with the design, fold the card, write your message inside and send it to a friend!

## MATERIALS

Pattern paper • heavy white paper, such as construction paper • pencil • tape • a large sewing needle • envelope

# St Nick Card Holder

## MATERIALS

One large can • green and white wool • glue • white posterboard or heavy paper • scissors • red, pink, white, blue and black felt

After you begin receiving cards in the post, it is fun to have a special place to put them where you can read them again and again. If you make this St Nick card holder, you will always have a fun way to keep your cards!

**1** Ask an adult to cut the top and bottom from the can (without leaving sharp edges). Wrap the sides from top to bottom with the green and white wool. Glue the ends firmly.

**2** Cut a circle from the white posterboard that you can make into a cone to fit on top of the can for the head. Cut slits around the bottom edge to help you stick it to the can.

**3** Use the felt to cut out the face pieces and hands and to wrap around the cone top to make a hat. When you are ready to use the card holder, open your cards and slip them through the wool.

# SWEETS AND TREATS

M mmmm! What would Christmas be without sweets and treats to share and enjoy? Your family might already have special things that you always eat during holiday times. If they don't, maybe some of the recipes here will be a new tradition at your house! Some of these recipes would be good to make and give as gifts, but all of them are just good to eat.

Remember, always wash your hands well before you begin to mix and cook, to lay out all of your ingredients before you start, and to clean up your mess when you are through! If you aren't sure how you can wrap up your food gift, check the chapter in this book called "Wrap It Up."

# Caramel Popcorn Balls

popcorn and stir well. To make the popcorn balls extra-special, you can add small candies or nuts to the popcorn before you pour the syrup on.

## INGREDIENTS

- 8 cups of popcorn
- ¾ cup white sugar
- ¾ cup brown sugar, packed
- ½ cup light corn syrup
- ½ cup water
- 1 teaspoon white vinegar
- ¾ cup butter

**1** Pour the popcorn into a large bowl. Put all of the ingredients except the butter into a saucepan. Bring to a boil over a medium heat, stirring constantly! When the temperature reaches 260° Fahrenheit. turn the heat down.

**3** Let the mixture cool slightly. Then butter your hands and form the coated popcorn into balls. Put the balls on wax paper to cool and harden. When the balls are cooled off, wrap them in clear cellophane or plastic wrap, tie with a bow and place them in a bowl where everyone can help themselves.

**2** Add the butter and stir until it has melted. Pour the hot mixture over the

# Cheesy Spread

## INGREDIENTS

1 x 227g package of cream cheese
½ cup butter
2 cloves of minced garlic
4 tablespoons of chopped parsley

**1** Soften the cream cheese to room temperature and mix all of the ingredients together until they are smooth and well blended.

**2** Place in a 550ml crock and serve with bread or crackers. Be sure to keep this cheese spread in the refrigerator until you are going to eat it.

# Lollipop Biscuits

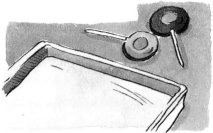

**1** Set the oven to 375° Fahrenheit. Spread aluminium foil over two baking sheets and unwrap the lollipops.

**2** Take the dough out of the refrigerator just before you slice it – it needs to be very cold! Cut the dough into 24 slices.

**3** Cut the centre of the biscuits out about the size of the lollipops with a small knife. Place the biscuits about 5cm apart on the baking sheets and set the lollipops into the centre. Set the cut-out circles on the biscuit sheets too – you can just bake and eat these! Bake the biscuits for about 10–15 minutes or until they are golden brown. Let the biscuits cool off before you peel them from the foil and eat them!

## INGREDIENTS

1 x 454g roll of refrigerated biscuit dough, or your own refrigerator biscuit dough recipe made up •
24 flat, thin lollipops (about 2.5cm diameter) with a cloth-type handle

# Scotch Shortbread

## INGREDIENTS

- ¾ cup soft butter
- ¼ cup sugar
- 2 cups flour

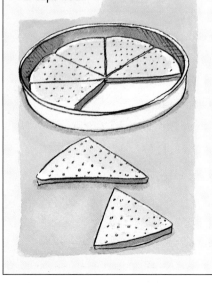

**1** Set your oven to 350° Fahrenheit. Cream the butter and sugar together, then work in the flour. If the dough seems to be crumbly, add 1 or 2 additional tablespoons of soft butter.

**2** Put the dough into a round cake pan, patting evenly so that the dough goes to the edges of the pan. Use a fork to poke holes all over the dough and bake it for about 20 minutes.

**3** Take the shortbread out of the oven and cut it into wedge-shaped pieces. Remove from the pan and cool.

# Melted Sweets Wreaths

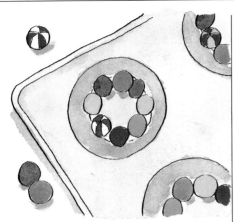

**1** Place the hard sweets all around the edges of the cake tins, so that the sweets are touching. Leave the centre of the cake tin open.

**2** Place the cake tins in a preheated oven (about 325° Fahrenheit) for about 5 or 6 minutes or until you can see the sweets begin to melt together.

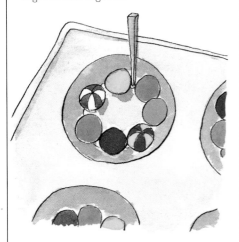

**3** Remove the cake tins from the oven and poke a hole at the top of each wreath with the skewer.

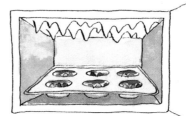

**4** Place the cake tins in the freezer part of your refrigerator for a few minutes.

**5** Remove the wreaths by pressing on the backs of the cake tins with your thumbs.

**6** To preserve the melted sweets wreaths, spray them with a preservative and attach a thread for hanging. You could glue a ribbon on at the top or bottom if you like!

## INGREDIENTS

- Hard sweets
- 7cm cake tins or other small baking pans
- A sharp object, such as a skewer
- Preservative spray
- Fine thread for hanging
- Ribbon (optional)

# JUST FOR FUN

*I*s Christmas your favourite time of the year? There are so many things to do to get ready for Christmas! It's so important to have fun with all the things you do before and during Christmas. Here are some things to do 'just for fun' as you get ready to celebrate Christmas Day.

# Pine Cone Basket

A pine cone basket makes a great gift-holder, but is a great gift too!

**I** Starting at the bottom of the basket, begin gluing pine cones around the bottom and work your way up to the rim. You will have to hold each pine cone in place for a moment after you glue it to make sure the glue has set.

**2** When the glue is dry, wrap the ribbon around the handle and tie it in a bow.

**3** If you haven't used a basket with a handle, tie the ribbon into a bow and glue to the basket for a decoration.

## MATERIALS

A basket you like; with or without a handle • pine cones about the same size • glue gun or heavy-duty glue that sticks to many surfaces • ribbon

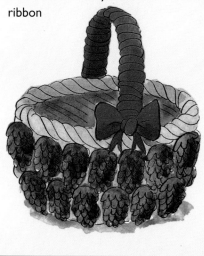

# Gumdrop Houses

## MATERIALS

Cardboard boxes • masking tape • gumdrops and other sweets • glue or stiff icing • tubes and other containers

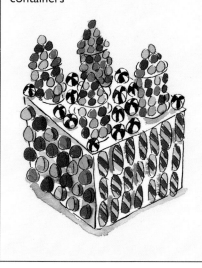

You can make a different type of 'gingerbread' house with gumdrops and sweets of all sorts.

**I** Start by taping your containers together into a house or castle shape. Be creative!

**2** Then experiment with your gumdrops and sweets to decide where you will put them on your house. When you think you are ready, spread glue or icing on the containers and begin building the outside of the house.

**3** This house is not one that you can eat, but of course, it won't hurt to nibble a sweet or two during the construction process!

# Bird Biscuit Houses

Use your imagination to make a 'home tweet home' for imaginary birds on a shelf or in your Christmas tree.

**1** Collect your materials. If you want to use a box or container as the base, fasten the edges together firmly. If you want to begin with crackers or biscuits, use the stiff icing along the edges to 'build' a simple square or rectangle as your base.

**2** Decide how you will decorate your bird house and then spread a layer of stiff icing along the outside, pressing nuts and other items into the icing as trim.

**3** You can make a bird perch by using icing to fasten a biscuit to the front of the house sticking out, and you can cut a hole above the perch for the bird to fly in and out!

## MATERIALS

Small boxes or containers for the base • crackers • biscuits • stiff icing • nuts • assorted decorating trims such as slivered almonds or other nuts • raisins and small sweets

# Bottle Top Wreath

## MATERIALS

A collection of bottle tops (metal or plastic) approximately all the same size • assorted fabrics (all the same colour or different colours and patterns) • scissors • needle and thread • ribbon

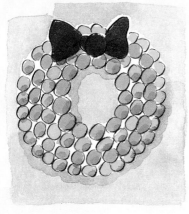

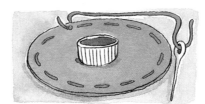

**1** Cut a circle of fabric that will fit around each of your bottle tops with room to spare. To fasten, you will need to set the bottle top in the middle of the fabric circle and pull the edges together at the back with a running stitch.

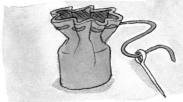

**2** When you have enclosed the bottle tops, use a needle and thread to attach the circles together by taking a tiny stitch in the fabrics of two circle edges.

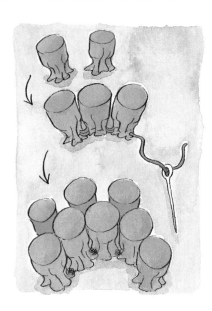

**3** You will need about 14 circles sewn together in the centre for the wreath. Keep adding circles to the outside to make the wreath as large as you want. Add a bow when you are finished.

# Pine Cone Growing Tree

1 Soak several pine cones in water briefly,
then roll the cones in grass seed.

2 Prop the cones on the bottom of a
saucer or shallow bowl, leaving a thin
layer of water in the bottom of the saucer.

3 Put it in a light place, wait a week or so
and watch your 'tree' begin to grow
green!

# Pine Cone Angel

they fasten into the pine cone and so that
the halo stands above the angel's head.

3 Cut the angel's wings from paper and
glue into either side of the cone. If you
want your angel to be a Christmas tree
decoration, you can add a thread to her back
so that she flies!

1 If you like, you can paint the entire pine
cone white, or just the tips. Glue the
wooden bead or foam ball to the top of the
pine cone for the head. Glue yarn hair on the
top of the bead, and draw a face with your
felt-pens.

2 Twist the pipe cleaner into a circle for
the halo, bending the ends down so that

# Mistletoe Ring

**1** Wrap the wreath or ring with the wide ribbon, covering all of it and securing the ends with glue. Use other pieces of ribbon to wrap and tie between the ribbon already wrapped, so that you can fill in any spaces.

**2** Use more ribbon to tie from four sides and fasten at the top for hanging.

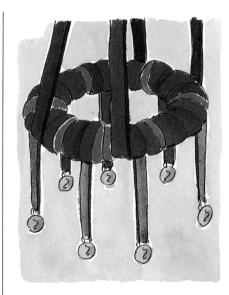

**3** Let some of the ribbons hang down so that you can tie or glue jingle bells to the ends of them. Hang the mistletoe from the inside of the wreath. Be sure to hang your mistletoe ring where lots of people can meet underneath it!

## MATERIALS

A foam or vine wreath · 8 metres of 4cm wide ribbon · glue · assorted colours and lengths of ribbons · scissors · jingle bells · mistletoe

# Twig Star

## MATERIALS

Small twigs and branches that are dry · wire or heavy-duty glue · white, silver or gold paint (optional) · glitter (optional)

**1** Arrange six twigs or small dry branches into two triangle shapes approximately the same size. Fasten the triangles together with wire or glue.

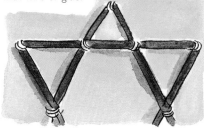

**2** Lay the triangles across each other as shown and fasten the triangles to each other with wire or glue.

**3** If you like, you can paint the star with white, silver or gold paint for added sparkle. When the paint is still wet, you might even want to sprinkle glitter on it for a real shine!

# A Wreath for the Birds

**1** Collect together the materials that you will need to make the wreath.

**2** Cover the wreath with moss, then wrap wire around the different kinds of bird treats you have collected and attach them to the wreath.

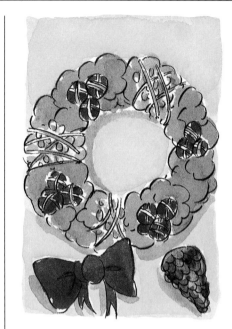

**3** Add a bow or pine cones if you like. Hang the wreath outside your front door, on a tree or an outside building where the birds will see it and begin to feast.

## MATERIALS

Wire or twig wreath • moss • assorted grains • sunflowers • leaves and berries that birds in your area like to eat • bow or pine cone (optional)

# Decorated Bird Tree

## MATERIALS

A tree • oranges, apples and other fruit • stale bread and biscuits • yarn or string • popcorn garlands

You can decorate an entire tree for the birds that frequent your yard or garden.

**1** Tie string or yarn to the pieces of fruit, stale bread and other treats and hang them from the tree branches.

**2** You could also wind old popcorn garlands around the tree. This is a good thing to do after Christmas Day when you are taking popcorn strings off your own tree. Birds like stale biscuits too!

# Stuffed Paper Gingerbread

## MATERIALS

Brown paper bags or wrapping paper · scissors · felt-pens · stapler · newspaper

**1** Draw a gingerbread boy or girl on a sheet of brown wrapping paper or the back of a brown paper bag. Cut two pieces of paper at once, so that you will have a double gingerbread person.

**2** Draw a face and other features such as a vest, bow tie or other clothing on one

side of the gingerbread person, then sandwich the two shapes together and begin to staple around the edges to close them up.

**3** Leave a small opening along one side so that you can stuff crumpled up newspaper inside. When the gingerbread boy or girl is 'plump', finish stapling the shape all the way around.

# Christmas Guest Book

**1** Why not start a special family tradition by having a guest book that everyone who visits your home during the holidays can sign?

| Katie | 21.12.94 |
|-------|----------|
| Mark  | 23.12.94 |

**2** Make sure they put the date and maybe even draw a picture or two along with their names.

| Name | Date |
|--------|----------|
| Leo | 2.10.93 |
| Jane | 20.10.93 |
| Mathew | 16.11.93 |
| Chloe | 29.11.93 |
| Peter | 1.12.9 |

**3** It will be fun to look back over the years and see who your Christmas visitors were!

## MATERIALS

A guest book · notebook or paper you have stapled together to make a book · felt-pens

| Name | Date | Notes |
|---------|---------|-----------|
| Grandad | 15.12.94 | Lovely time |
| Auntie | 21.12.94 | super! |
| Katie | 21.12.94 | really |
| Mark | 23.12.94 | Good fun xx |

# Tissue Paper Windows

## MATERIALS

Black construction paper or other heavy paper · pencil · scissors · a variety of coloured tissue paper · glue

**1** Trace a simple window shape design on a piece of black paper with a pencil. Lay another piece of black paper behind it and cut the window shape out of both pieces of paper.

**2** Cut and glue pieces of coloured tissue paper in the open window spaces on one piece of paper.

**3** When you are pleased with your window, glue the other piece of black paper to the first, so that the tissue paper is sandwiched in between. When the glue dries, hang your paper window in another window and watch the colour shine through.

# Holiday Greeting Welcome Mat

**1** Collect together the materials you need to make your Welcome Mat.

**2** Decide what your design will be and sketch it on the mat.

**3** Fill in the design with brightly coloured paints. Let it dry. Put the finished mat just inside or outside a main door to your house so that everyone will feel welcome when they arrive.

## MATERIALS

A door mat or carpet square · paint brush · acrylic or other durable paint